Emma Szlachta

Super Grammar

Practice Book Level 1

CAMBRIDGE
UNIVERSITY PRESS

Contents

Numbers

Super Grammar

Use **How old are you?** and **I'm ...** to ask and answer about ages.

How old are you?   **I'm** *nine.*
                             I'm *ten.*

1   **Match the numbers.**

How old are you?

2 Follow the numbers in the maze.

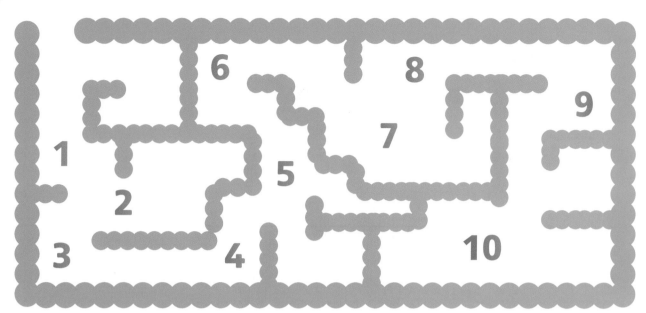

3 Write the numbers.

1   2   3

one   _____   _____

4   5

_____   _____

6   7   8

_____   _____   _____

9   10

_____   _____

Colours

I'm Ned. My hat is blue.

I'm Ben. My hat is green.

I'm Alice. My hat is purple.

Super Grammar

Use **colours** to describe different objects.
A **red** hat.   My hat is **green**.

1 **Match the colours with the words.**

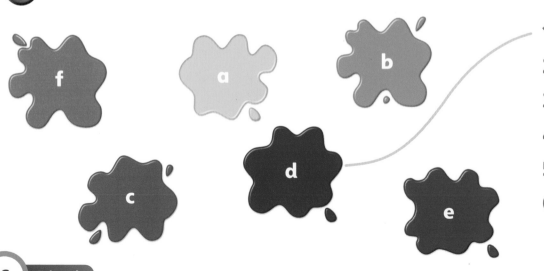

1 blue

2 orange

3 yellow

4 red

5 green

6 purple

2 **Write the letters to complete the colours.**

1 gr_e__e_n   2 o__a____e   3 r_____

4 ___ur__l   5 ____e____l__w   6 b____e

3 **Write the colours.**

1 A _____blue_____ balloon.   2 A _____ balloon.

3 A _____ balloon.   4 A _____ balloon.

5 A _____ balloon.   6 An _____ balloon.

Reading: a chat

1 Read the conversation and match the phrases.

1 Sally   **a** seven

2 Hugo   **b** Green

3 Sally is   **c** eight

4 Hugo is   **d** Black

Writing

2 Write the questions.

1   you / old / How / are / ?

_____

2   your / name / What's / ?

_____

3 Write a chat with a friend. Draw pictures.

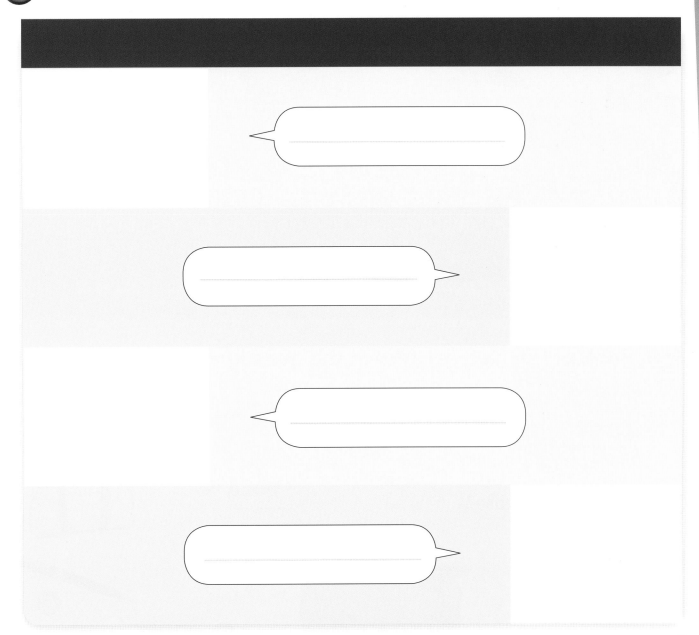

1 Questions and short answers

 What's this? Is it a bag?

What's this? Is it a pencil?

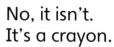 Is it a pencil?

Yes, it is. It's a purple pencil.

 Yes, it is.

No, it isn't. It's a crayon.

Super Grammar

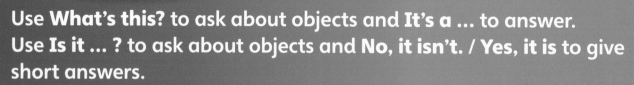

Use **What's this?** to ask about objects and **It's a ...** to answer.
Use **Is it ... ?** to ask about objects and **No, it isn't.** / **Yes, it is** to give short answers.

What's this? *It's a pencil.* *Is it a pen?* *No, it isn't. / Yes, it is.*

1 **Look at the pictures. Match the questions with the responses.**

1   Is it a rubber?
2   Is it a pencil?
3   Is it a desk?
4   Is it a pencil case?
5   Is it a ruler?
6   Is it a bag?

Yes, it is.

No, it isn't.

2 Match the questions with the responses.

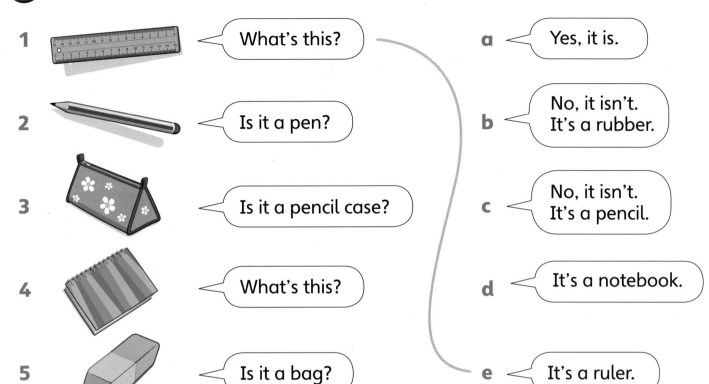

1. What's this?
2. Is it a pen?
3. Is it a pencil case?
4. What's this?
5. Is it a bag?

a Yes, it is.
b No, it isn't. It's a rubber.
c No, it isn't. It's a pencil.
d It's a notebook.
e It's a ruler.

3 Write questions and answers.

1 this / What's / ?

   What's this ?

   a / It's / desk / .

   _____ .

2 rubber / it / Is / a / ?

   _____ ?

   is / Yes, / it / .

   _____ .

3 it / notebook / Is / a / ?

   _____ ?

   isn't / it / No, / .

   _____ .

4 this / What's / ?

   _____ ?

   a / It's / bag / green / .

   _____ .

5 this / What's / ?

   _____ ?

   a / desk / yellow / It's / .

   _____ .

Imperatives

Sit at your desk, please.

Open your bag, please.

Take out your pen, please.

Put away your bag, please.

Super Grammar

Use **imperatives** to give instructions.

Open your book, please.
Sit at your desk, please.
Put away your book, please.

Pass me a ruler, please.
Close your bag, please.
Take out your ruler, please.

---

1 **Match the sentences with the pictures.**

1 Close your bag, please. `b`   **4** Pass me a pen, please. ☐

2 Pass me a ruler, please. ☐   **5** Take out your ruler, please. ☐

3 Take out your book, please. ☐   **6** Open your bag, please. ☐

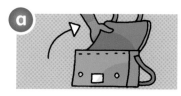

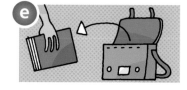

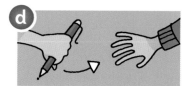

2 Complete the sentences with the words from the box.

Put   Turn   Pass   Open   away   ~~Pass~~

1 *Pass* me a pencil, please.

2 _____ your books, please.

3 _____ around.

4 _____ your rubber on your head.

5 _____ me a ruler, please.

6 Put _____ your bags, please.

3 Look and write.

1 Open *your bags,* please.

2 Sit at _____.

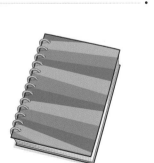

3 Close _____, please.

4 Pass _____, please.

5 Take _____, please.

6 Put _____, please.

Reading: a comic strip

1 **Read the text and draw lines.**

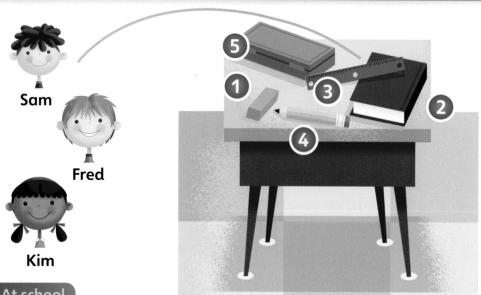

Writing

2 **What objects are on your desk and in your classroom?**

a black book

_____ _____ _____

_____ _____ _____

3 **Write a story. Draw pictures.**

What's his name?

His name is Ben.

How old is he?

He's six.

What's his favourite toy?

His favourite toy's his ball.

What's her name?

Her name is Grace. She's seven and her favourite toy is a ball too!

Super Grammar

Asking and answering questions using **his**, **her**, **he** and **she**.

*What's **his** name?*	***His** name's Ned.*
*How old is **he**?*	***He's** six.*
*What's **his** favourite toy?*	***His** favourite toy's his ball.*
*What's **her** name?*	***Her** name's Alice.*
*How old is **she**?*	***She's** eight.*
*What's **her** favourite toy?*	***Her** favourite toy's her kite.*

1 **Match the questions with the responses.**

1	What's her name?	a	He's ten.
2	What's her favourite toy?	b	His name's Tim.
3	How old is she?	c	Her name's Kim.
4	What's his favourite toy?	d	She's six.
5	What's his name?	e	Her favourite toy's her bike.
6	How old is he?	f	His favourite toy's his plane.

2 Complete the sentences with the words from the box.

favourite ~~her~~ She's What's name she

1 What's _her_ name?   Her _____'s Sophie

2 _____ her favourite toy?   Her _____ toy's her go-kart.

3 How old is _____ ?   _____ seven.

3 Write questions and answers.

1 his / What's / name / ?   What's his name?
  Ben / His / name's / .   _____.

2 Toby / How / old / is / ?   _____?
  seven / He's / .   _____.

3 his / What's / number / favourite / ?   _____?
  number / favourite / is / His / ten / .   _____.

4 her / What's / name / ?   _____?
  name's / Mary / Her / .   _____.

Adjectives

It's a big yellow plane.

It's a long red train.

It's a new black go-kart.

It's an ugly orange monster!

Super Grammar

Use **an** before words beginning with **a, e, i, o** or **u** (vowels).

It's **a new** kite.

It's **a long blue** train.

It's **an ugly** monster.

It's **a big green** ball.

1 **Read and tick (✓) or cross (✗).**

1 It's a long red train   ✗
2 It's a big green ball.
3 It's an ugly blue monster.
4 It's a new pink go-kart.
5 It's a long blue train.
6 It's a big yellow ball.

2 **Circle the correct words to complete the sentences.**

1 It's (a) / *an* short green train.

2 It's *a* / *an* ugly purple monster.

3 It's a *beautiful new* / *new beautiful* doll.

4 It's *a* / *an* small yellow ball.

5 It's a *green big* / *big green* monster.

6 It's *a* / *an* old black go-kart.

3 **Write sentences with *a* / *an* and the words from the box.**

~~yellow bike~~   ugly green monster   yellow and red plane
beautiful doll   blue car   big ball

1 It's *a yellow bike* .

2 It's _____ .

3 It's _____ .

4 It's _____ .

5 It's _____ .

6 It's _____ .

Reading: an email

1 **Read the text and answer the questions.**

•••

To: Ana
From: Tom

Hi Ana

I'm Tom and I'm seven. My favourite toy's my yellow go-kart. It's new! Look – this is my go-kart!

What's your favourite toy? How old are you?

Tom

•••

To: Tom
From: Ana

Hi Tom

I'm seven. My favourite toy isn't a doll or a computer game. My favourite toy's my bike. It's a new green bike. My favourite colour's green. Look – this is my bike! What's your favourite colour?

Ana

1 What's his name?

His name's Tom.

2 How old is he?

3 What's his favourite toy?

4 What's her name?

5 What colour is her bike?

6 What's her favourite colour?

Writing

2 **Write answers.**

What's your favourite toy? _____

What isn't your favourite toy? _____

What colour is it? _____

Is it new or old? _____

3 **Write an email to Tom or Ana. Use your notes from Exercise 2. Draw a picture of the toy.**

To:

From:

3 In, on, under

The dog is under the desk.   The cat is on the desk.   The rat is in the bag.

Super Grammar

Use **prepositions** to describe where things are.

	in	
The lizard is	**on**	**the bag.**
	under	

1 **Match the sentences with the pictures.**

1 The cat is under the desk. [b]

2 The frog is in the bag. [ ]

3 The lizard is on the bag. [ ]

4 The lizard is in the pencil case. [ ]

5 The rat is under the desk. [ ]

2 **Write *in*, *on* or *under*. Draw lines.**

1 The rats are ___in___ the desk.

2 The ducks are _____ on the books.

3 The elephants are _____ the ruler.

4 The cats are _____ the desk.

5 The lizards are _____ the bag.

6 The spiders are _____ the pencil case.

3 **Look and write.**

1 The spider is in the pencil case.

2 _____

3 _____

4 _____

5 _____

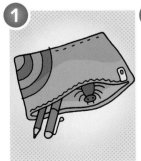

I like/I don't like ...

Super Grammar

Use **like** and **don't like** to express likes and dislikes.

😊 *I like dogs.*

😊 *I like dogs too.*

☹ *I don't like dogs.*

1 Circle the correct words to complete the sentences.

1   I *like* / *don't like* dogs.
2   I *like* / *don't like* ducks.
3   I *like* / *don't like* cats.
4   I *like* / *don't like* frogs.
5   I *like* / *don't like* rats.

2 **Complete the sentences with the words from the box.**

> too   like   green   ~~like~~   don't   lizards

Ben I ¹___like___ dogs.

Tim I like dogs ²_____ .

Ben I ³_____ like rats. What about you?

Tim I like rats and I ⁴_____ lizards.

Ben I like ⁵_____ too – they are my favourite – big ⁶_____ lizards!

3 **Look and write.**

 ☺

 ☹

1   _I like cats._

2   _____

 ☺

 ☹

3   _____

4   _____

 ☺

 ☹

5   _____

6   _____

Reading: a project

1 **Look at the pictures. Read the texts and choose *yes* or *no*.**

This is my cat. His name is Felix. He's nine.
His favourite toy's his doll. Felix is a small
brown and black cat. He's in my bag!
I like cats – cats are my favourite.
I don't like dogs. What about you?

Sophie

This is my rat. Her name is Rita.
She's five. Her favourite toy's her ball.
Rita is a small white rat. I like rats
– rats are my favourite. I don't like
cats. What about you?

Max

1	Felix is a rat.	*yes* / (*no*)
2	Felix's favourite toy is his doll.	*yes* / *no*
3	Felix is on the bag.	*yes* / *no*
4	Rita is five.	*yes* / *no*
5	Her favourite toy is her doll.	*yes* / *no*
6	She is black and white.	*yes* / *no*

Writing

2 **Write the sentences.**

1 nine / is / years / old. / Digby

_____

2 is / white. / He / black / and

_____

3 ball. / favourite / His / a toy / toy / is

_____

3 **Write about Digby. Use the sentences from Exercise 2.**

I've got/
I haven't got ...

I've got a cheese sandwich.

I haven't got a cheese sandwich.

I've got a cake.

I haven't got a cake.

I've got an apple.

Me too! I've got a big green apple.

Super Grammar

Use **have got** and **haven't got** to talk about possessions.

I've got a sandwich and an apple.
I haven't got a banana.

1 **Look and write *yes* or *no*.**

1   I've got a cake.   yes
2   I've got bananas.   _____
3   I've got pizza.   _____
4   I haven't got peas.   _____
5   I haven't got chicken.   _____
6   I've got orange juice.   _____

2 **Complete the sentences with the words from the box.**

Me ~~got~~ too got 've haven't

1 I've got a kiwi. | Me too!

2 I've got pizza. | I _____ got pizza. I've got chicken.

3 I've got a cake. | Me _____ !

4 What's for lunch? | I haven't _____ chicken. I've got sausages.

5 I've got meatballs and peas. | I _____ got meatballs but I haven't got peas. I've got carrots.

6 I've got a cheese sandwich. | _____ too!

3 **Look and write.**

1 I haven't got a cake. 2 _____

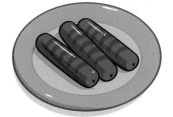

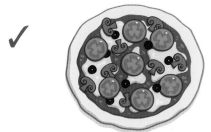

3 _____ 4 _____

Have ... got any ... ?

Have we got any cheese?

No, we haven't.

Have we got any cake?

No, we haven't.

Have we got any sausages?

No, we haven't. We've got pizza.

Hooray! I like pizza.

Super Grammar

Use **Have ... got any ...?** to ask about possessions.
Use **Yes, we have** and **No, we haven't** to give short answers.

Have we **got any** cheese?   **Yes, we have.**
                                     No, we haven't.

---

1 **Look at the pictures. Match the questions with the responses.**

1   Have we got any apples?

2   Have we got any bananas?

3   Have we got any orange juice?

4   Have we got any sausages?

5   Have we got any cheese?

6   Have we got any chicken?

Yes, we have.   No, we haven't.

2 Write the dialogue in the correct order.

Have you got sausage on your pizza?

Me too! I like sausages.

No, I haven't. I don't like carrots. I've got cheese.

Yes, I have. I've got cheese and sausage. Sausage is my favourite.

Have you got carrots on your pizza?

Alice Have you got carrots on your pizza?

Katy _____

Alice _____

Katy _____

Alice _____

3 Write questions.

1 Have we got any apples?   2 _____

3 _____   4 _____

5 _____   6 _____

Reading: a text message

1 **Read. Tick (✓) the food in the text messages.**

sausage ✓   steak ☐   chicken ☐   pizza ☐
carrots ☐   peas ☐   bananas ☐   apples ☐
sandwich ☐   apple juice ☐   orange juice ☐   milk ☐

● ● ● ○ ○   7.05 pm

> Hi May! I'm at the shop. I haven't got my shopping list. Look in the kitchen and help me please! Have we got any cheese?

Hi Mum! Yes, we have.

> OK. Have we got any bananas and apples?

We've got one banana. We haven't got any apples.

> Have we got chicken?

No. We haven't got chicken but we've got eight sausages and we haven't got pizza – pizza's my favourite!

> OK, May! A cheese pizza too!

2 **Write the food words.**

We haven't got any ¹ _apples_ but we've
got one ² _____ and we've got ³ _____ .
We haven't got any ⁴ _____ or ⁵ _____
but we've got eight ⁶ _____

Writing

3 **Look and write the food.**

cheese

_____   _____

_____   _____

_____   _____

_____   _____

4 **Look. Write a dialogue about the picture in Exercise 3.**

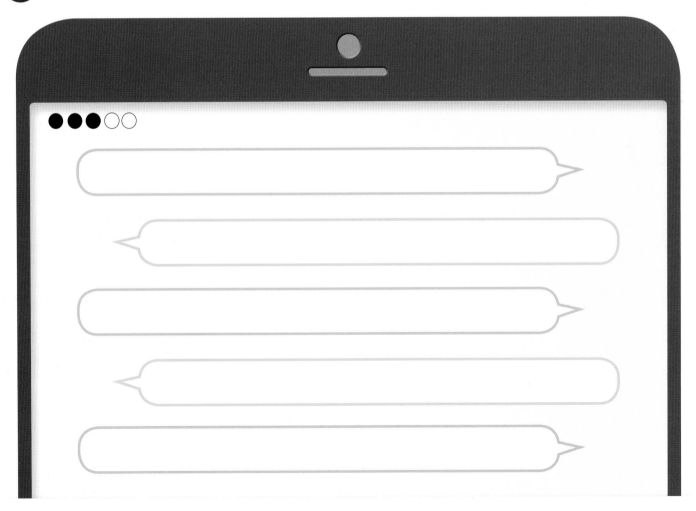

5 Free time

On Thursdays I play football. What about you?

I go to school on Saturdays.

It's OK. School is cool.

I go swimming on Thursdays. I play football on Saturdays. What do you do on Saturdays?

On Saturday?!

Super Grammar

Use the verbs **go ...** and **play ...** to talk about free time activities.

I **go swimming** on Mondays.
I **play football** on Saturdays.

1 **Match the sentences with the pictures.**

1 On Mondays I ride my bike. ☐d

2 On Fridays I play computer games. ☐

3 I go swimming on Thursdays. ☐

4 'What do you do on Sundays?' 'I watch TV and sleep!' ☐

5 I play football with friends on Saturdays. ☐

6 On Tuesdays I play with my toys. ☐

2 **Circle the correct words to complete the sentences.**

1 I (play) / go football on Saturdays.

2 I play / go swimming on Fridays.

3 What do you do / go on Thursdays?

4 I ride / play my pony on Sundays.

5 I do / play computer games on Tuesdays.

6 I do / play the piano on Wednesdays.

3 **Write sentences with the words from the boxes and days.**

go   play   ride   watch

~~football~~   computer games   swimming   TV   ball   bike

1 I play football on Tuesdays.

2 _____

3 _____

4 _____

5 _____

6 _____

Tuesday

Monday

Saturday

Thursday

Friday

Sunday

Do you ... ? Yes, I do./ No, I don't.

Do you watch TV at the weekend?

No, I don't.

Yes, I do.

Do you play computer games at the weekend?

Super Grammar

Use **Do you ... ?** to ask about activities. Use **Yes, I do** and **No, I don't** to give short answers.

Do you watch TV at the weekend?
No, I don't.
Do you play in the park at the weekend?
Yes, I do.

1 **Write *Yes, I do* or *No, I don't*.**

1   Do you watch TV at the weekend?   ✗   No, I don't.
2   Do you play with your toys on Sundays?   ✓   _____
3   Do you play football at the weekend?   ✗   _____
4   Do you ride your bike on Tuesdays?   ✓   _____
5   Do you play in the park at the weekend?   ✓   _____
6   Do you go swimming on Fridays?   ✗   _____

2 **Match the sentences with the pictures.**

1 Do you watch TV at the weekend? `c`
  Yes, I do.

2 Do you play computer games on Fridays? ☐
  Yes, I do.

3 Do you play computer games at the weekend? ☐
  No, I don't. I play football.

4 Do you watch TV on Sundays? ☐
  No, I don't. I read a book.

5 Do you play hide-and-seek at the weekend? ☐
  No, I don't. I sing with my friends.

6 Do you play football on Sundays? ☐
  Yes, I do.

3 **Write the questions.**

1 ride / Do / you / at the weekend / your / bike / ?

  Do you ride your bike at the weekend?

2 Do / football / you / on Sundays / play / ?

  _____?

3 go / you / at the weekend / swimming / Do / ?

  _____?

4 you / hide-and-seek / play / on Saturdays / Do / ?

  _____?

5 watch / at the weekend / you / Do / TV / ?

  _____?

6 Do / the piano / play / you / on Mondays / ?

  _____?

Reading: a blog

 1 **Read the blog. Write Sam's diary.**

MyBlog

Sam Brown
My week

It's a busy week for me! On Monday I play tennis for one hour and on Tuesday I swim for one hour. On Wednesday and Friday I watch TV and read a book. On Thursday I ride my bike with my friend Meg – we ride our bikes for two hours. Saturday is my favourite day! I go to the park and play with my friends – we play football. On Sunday I watch TV and play computer games. What do you do at the weekend?

Monday	Friday
play tennis	
Tuesday	Saturday
Wednesday	Sunday
Thursday	

Writing

2 **Write your diary.**

Monday	Friday
play tennis	
Tuesday	Saturday
Wednesday	Sunday
Thursday	

3 **Write a blog. Use your diary in Exercise 2 to help you. Draw your picture.**

MyBlog

⑥ There's/There are ...

There's a frog under the log.

Cool!

There are two beautiful butterflies on the flower.

There's a big scary spider in the tree.

Cool!

There's ... a monster under the table. Aagh! Oh, it's Spot!

Super Grammar

Use **there is** and **there are** to say what singular and plural nouns you can see.

***There's** a monster.*   ***There are** four cats.*
***There's** a frog.*   ***There are** three apples on the tree.*

1 Match the words with the pictures.

a

b

c

d

e

f

There are

There is

2 **Write *There is* or *There are*.**

1 *There is* a cat in the living room.

2 _____ five frogs in my bedroom.

3 _____ a cat on the TV.

4 _____ a frog in my bedroom.

5 _____ a monster under the table.

6 _____ two cats in the dining room.

3 **Look and write.**

1 *There is a snake in the cellar.*
(a snake / cellar)

2 _____ .
(a lizard / bedroom)

3 _____ .
(seven crocodiles / bathroom)

4 _____ .
(five tigers / garden)

5 _____ .
(a spider / kitchen)

6 _____ .
(a cat / living room)

Is there/Are there ... ?/ How many ... ?

Are there any bikes?

No, there aren't.

How many cars are there?

There are ten cars.

Is there a plane?

Yes, there is!

Super Grammar

Use **Is there ... ?** to ask about singular nouns. Use **Are there ...?** to ask about plural nouns. Use **Yes, there is** and **No, there isn't** to give short answers.

Use **How many ... are there?** to ask about a plural number of things. Use **There are ...** to give an answer about plural nouns.

Is there a plane?   Yes, *there is.*
Are there any rats?   *No*, there aren't.
How many cars are there?   *There are* four cars.

1 **Circle the correct words to complete the sentences.**

1   Are / Is there any pears?

2   Are / Is there any rats?

3   How many cars *are / is* there?

4   Are / Is there a plane?

5   Are / Is there a go-kart?

6   How many cakes *are / is* there?

2 **Look and write answers.**

1 Is there a cat? *Yes, there is.*

2 Are there any balls? _____

3 Is there a frog? _____

4 How many sausages are there? _____

5 Is there a go-kart? _____

6 How many apples are there? _____

 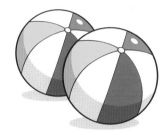 

3 **Complete the questions and answers.**

1 *Are there any* bikes? *Yes, there are.*

2 _____ cars? Yes, _____ .

3 _____ are there? _____ eight kites.

4 _____ a plane? _____ .

5 _____ a park? _____ .

6 _____ are there? _____ one cake.

Reading: a project

1 Read the text and the sentences. Write *yes* or *no*.

I live in a big house. It isn't old, it's new. There are four bedrooms, a kitchen, a dining room, a living room and a hall. My bedroom is my favourite room. It's blue. There are posters of animals and I've got a green rug. There's a desk in my bedroom and I've got a computer. There isn't a TV. My toys are in my bedroom and my teddy bear is on my bed. I play with my toys at the weekend.

1   The house is small.   no

2   There are five bedrooms.

3   The rug is blue.

4   There isn't a computer.

5   There's a TV in the bedroom.

6   There are toys in the bedroom.

Writing

2 **Make notes about your house and bedroom.**

Rooms	My bedroom	Adjectives

3 **Draw and write about your house and your bedroom.**

7

Do you like this/these ... ?

Do you like this hat?

Do you like this jacket?

Do you like these shoes?

Do you like these jeans?

Yes, I do!

No, I don't! Put on these shoes.

No, I don't! Put on this jacket.

Yes, I do!

Super Grammar

Use **Do you like this ... ?** to ask about singular nouns.
Use **Do you like these ... ?** to ask about plural nouns.
Use **Yes, I do** and **No, I don't** to give short answers.

Do you like this hat?   **Yes, I do.**
Do you like these shoes?   **No, I don't.**

1 **Match the words with the pictures.**

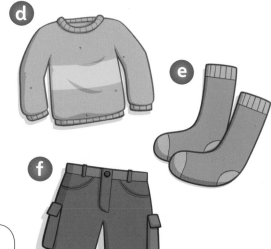

a   b   c   d   e   f

This   These

2 Write the questions.

1 this / Do / like / hat / you / ?   Do you like this hat?

2 these / you / shoes / Do / like / ?   ?

3 like / jacket / you / this / Do / ?   ?

4 like / you / shorts / these / Do / ?   ?

5 T-shirt / Do / you / like / this / ?   ?

6 you / jeans / like / Do / these / ?   ?

3 Look and write.

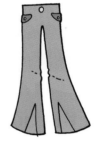

1 Do you ___like this hat___ ?
   ☺ Yes, ___I do___ .

2 Do you _____ ?
   ☹ No, _____ .

3 Do you _____ ?
   ☹ No, _____ .

4 Do _____ ?
   ☺ _____ .

5 Do _____ ?
   ☹ _____ .

6 _____ ?
   ☺ _____ .

Is he/she + -ing?

Where's James? Is he playing football?

Yes, he is.

That's James.

Is he wearing a black sweater?

No, he isn't. He's wearing a blue sweater.

Oh yes! I can see him.

Super Grammar

Use **Is he/she + -ing** to ask what people are doing.
Use **Yes, he is** and **No, she isn't** to give short answers.
Use **is + -ing** to describe what people are doing.

*Olivia's **wearing** a red sweater.*
*Is he **wearing** a blue T-shirt?*   ***Yes, he is.***
Is she wearing brown shoes?   ***No, she isn't.***

1 **Read the questions. Write _yes_ or _no_.**

1 Is Emma watching TV? _yes_

2 Is Paul playing a game? _____

3 Is Lara singing? _____

4 Is Ken playing a game? _____

5 Is Emma wearing a green T-shirt? _____

6 Is Ken wearing a blue sweater? _____

2 **Write Yes, he/she is or No, he/she isn't.**

1 Is he wearing red shorts?

Yes, he is.

2 Is he watching TV?

_____

3 Is he wearing a red sweater?

_____

4 Is she eating cake?

_____

5 Is he playing football?

_____

6 Is she playing computer games?

_____

3 **Write the questions and sentences.**

1 Anna / is / wearing / a blue skirt / .

Anna is wearing a blue skirt.

2 is / What / doing / Bob / ?

_____ ?

3 Are / Amy and Hannah / bikes / riding / ?

_____ ?

4 are / TV / watching / Emma and Tom / .

_____ .

5 playing / Oscar / football / is / .

_____ .

6 a sandwich / Kylie / Is / eating / ?

_____ ?

Reading: a chat

1 **Read the conversation and answer the questions.**

CHATS School friends	James, Amy

James Brown

> Hi Amy!

> I'm in my bedroom. I'm listening to music with my cat! He's on my bed!

Is he sleeping?

> Yes, he is.

Where are your mum and brother, Luke?

> My mum's in the dining room and Luke's in the living room.

Is your mum eating?

> No, she isn't. She's reading a book in her favourite chair!

Amy Little

1 Who is James talking to?

He's talking to Amy.

2 What is the cat doing?

_____

3 What is James doing?

_____

4 Where is Mum?

_____

5 Where is Luke?

_____

6 Is mum watching TV?

_____

Writing

2 **Make notes.**

You are at home. What are you doing?

_____

What is your mum doing? Where is she?

_____

Have you got a cat or a dog (what is he/she doing?)

_____

What is your brother/sister doing? Where is he/she?

_____

3 **Write a conversation with your friend.**

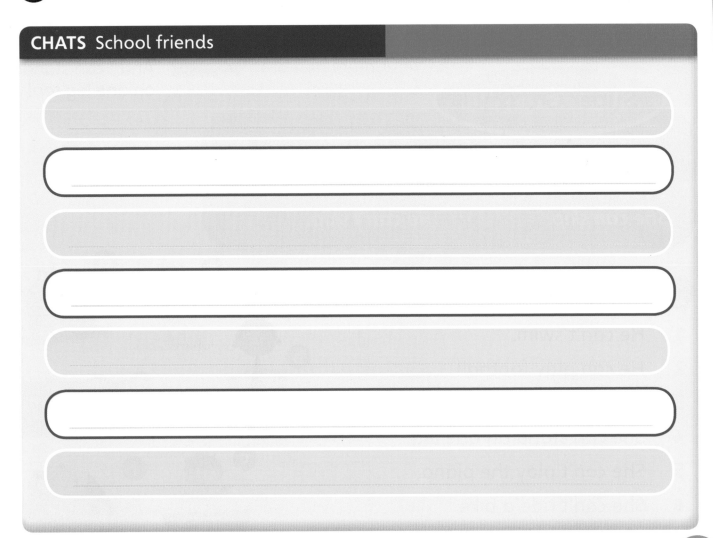

CHATS School friends

8 Can/can't for ability

I can skip.

I can't skip.

I can touch my toes.

I can't touch my toes.

I can stand on one leg.

I can stand on one leg.

And I can stand on one leg too!

Super Grammar

Use **can** and **can't** to talk about ability

I can stand on one leg.   **I can't** touch my toes.
She can skip.   **He can't** skip.

1 **Match the sentences with the pictures.**

1	He can't swim.	f
2	He can play football.	
3	He can skip.	
4	She can stand on one leg.	
5	She can't play the piano.	
6	She can't ride a bike.	

a

d

b

e

c

f

2 Write *can* or *can't*.

1

✗ He __can't__ swim.

2

✓ He _____ ride a horse.

3

✗ She _____ play tennis.

4

✗ He _____ play the piano.

5

✓ She _____ ride a bike.

6

✓ She _____ do ballet.

3 Look and write.

	Ned	Alice
(piano)	✗	✓
Hola	✗	✓
(guitar)	✓	✗

1 Ned can't play the piano.

4 _____

2 _____

5 _____

3 _____

6 _____

Questions with can

Super Grammar

Use **can** to ask about ability. Use **Yes, I can** and **No, I can't** to give short answers.

Can you swim?	*Yes, I can.*
Can you dance?	*No, I can't.*

1 **Match the questions with the responses.**

1	Can you dance?	**a**	I don't know. Let's see. Woah! No, I can't.
2	Can you fly a kite?	**b**	Yes, I can. I can play the piano too.
3	Can you ride a horse?	**c**	Yes, I can, and I can sing.
4	Can you stand on one leg?	**d**	No, I can't. I haven't got a kite.
5	Can you play the guitar?	**e**	Yes, I can. I swim at the weekends.
6	Can you swim?	**f**	No, I can't, but I can ride a bike.

2 **Complete the sentences with the words from the box.**

sing   speak   play   can   ~~yes~~   can't

Karl   Hello, May. Can you dance?

May   ¹ _Yes_ , I can.

Karl   Can you ² _____ the guitar?

May   No, I ³ _____ . But I can play the
piano and I can ⁴ _____ .

Karl   Can you ⁵ _____ Spanish?

May   No, I can't. But my sister ⁶ _____ .

3 **Write questions.**

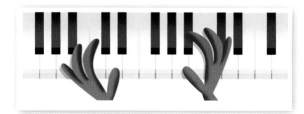

1   (piano) _Can you play the piano?_

No, I can't. But I can play the guitar.

2   (speak Spanish) _____

Yes, I can. ¡Hola!

3   (play tennis) _____

No, I can't. I can play football.

4   (ride a bike) _____

Yes, I can. My bike is pink.

5   (swim) _____

Yes, I can.

6   (ride a horse) _____

No, I can't. I don't like horses.

Reading: a forum

1   Read the text and write *yes* or *no*.

Pet forum

Super pets!

Alice

Can your cat sing?!

My cat is called Bob. He's black with one white foot! He's two years old. He can run and jump AND he can sing! What can your pet do?

Harry

Wow! No way! My cat can't sing. I've got a dog too. His name is Patch. He can swim and he can play football – we play football in the garden! Look at my photo.

Sally

Cool! I haven't got a cat or a dog, but I've got a horse. Her name is Jazzy. She's a big black horse – she's beautiful. She can't sing. She can jump up high, stand on two legs and she can skip.

1   Bob is one.   *no*

2   Bob can't sing.

3   Patch can swim.

4   Jazzy is a horse.

5   Jazzy is ugly.

6   Jazzy can skip and jump.

Writing

2 **Choose a pet and make notes.**

Pet

What's her/his name?

What colour is she/he?

How old is he/she?

She/he can

She/he can't

3 **Write a forum post. Use your notes from exercise 2 to help you.**

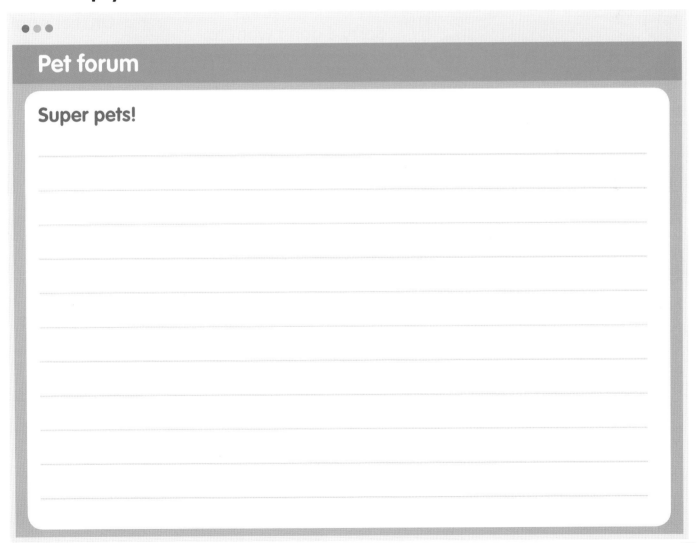

Pet forum

Super pets!

⑨ Suggestions

Super Grammar

Use **let's + verb** to make suggestions.

Let's play the guitar.   *Good idea.*
                              I'm not sure.
                              Sorry, I don't want to.

1 **Match the sentences with the pictures.**

1   Let's paint a picture.   d
2   Let's take a photo.   ☐
3   Let's look for shells.   ☐
4   Let's listen to music.   ☐
5   Let's go to the park.   ☐
6   Let's go swimming.   ☐

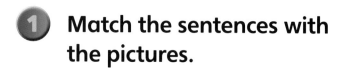

2 **Complete the sentences with the words from the box.**

Let's   idea   play   sure   eat   want

Hugo: ¹ _Let's_ look for shells.

Tony: I'm not ² _____.

Hugo: OK. Let's ³ _____ football.

Tony: Sorry, I don't ⁴ _____ to – we haven't got a ball.

Hugo: Let's ⁵ _____ an ice cream.

Tony: Good ⁶ _____. Banana is my favourite ice cream!

3 **Look and write.**

1   Let's play the guitar.

✓   Good idea.

2 _____

✗ Sorry, _____

3 _____

✓ _____

4 _____

✗ I'm _____

5 _____

✗ I'm _____

6 _____

✓ _____

Where's/Where are ... ?

Super Grammar

Use **Where's ...?** to ask about singular items.
Use **It's ...** to answer about singular items.
Use **Where are ...?** to ask about plural items.
Use **They're ...** to answer about singular items.

Where's the blue book?   **It's** in the green bag.
Where are the orange books?   **They're** in the black bag.

1 **Write the questions.**

1 are / Where / small / the / shells / ?   _Where are the small shells?_

2 is / the / dog / Where / big / ? _____?

3 are / blue / shoes / the / Where / ? _____?

4 the / Where / is / cat / ? _____?

5 beach / the / Where / is / ? _____?

6 orange / Where / the / are / kites / ? _____?

2 **Write answers.**

1 Where's the blue book?

It's in the green bag.

2 Where's the green lizard?

_____

3 Where are the green books?

_____

4 Where's the black spider?

_____

5 Where are the red books?

_____

6 Where's the yellow lizard?

_____

3 **Look. Complete the questions and answers.**

1 Where _'s the lizard_ ?
   _It's_ in the bedroom.

2 _____ the crocodiles?
   _____ in the bathroom.

3 _____ the cat?

room.

4 _____ the spider?

_____

5 _____ ?
It's in the cellar.

Reading: a magazine

1 **Read the text and answer the questions.**

Come to Wales

Wales is a beautiful country. There are lots of places to see. You can walk in the high mountains and swim in the sea at the beautiful beaches. There are lots of mountains, but go to Snowdon mountain – it's really high, so take your walking shoes! There are also lots of castles – go to famous Conwy Castle – it's very old. You can walk to the top of the castle and take photos of the mountains and the sea. You can see sheep too! Have lunch in the Castle café and eat Welsh cakes! Wales is fantastic!

Conwy Castle

Welsh cakes

1 What adjectives can you find? What do they describe?

beautiful country

2 What activities can you do on holiday in Wales?

3 What is the name of the high mountain?

4 What can you do at Conwy castle?

5 What animals can you see from the castle?

6 What food can you try?

Writing

2 **Match the phrases.**

1 walk up Ben Nevis   **a** bagpipe music

2 go to Edinburgh   **b** the Loch Ness monster

3 listen to   **c** haggis (meat with onion)

4 eat   **d** a mountain

5 look for shells on   **e** a city

6 find   **f** the fantastic beaches

3 **Write a magazine article about Scotland. Use the phrases in Exercise 2 to help you.**

Acknowledgements

The authors and publishers acknowledge the following sources of copyright material and are grateful for the permissions granted. While every effort has been made, it has not always been possible to identify the sources of all the material used, or to trace all copyright holders. If any omissions are brought to our notice, we will be happy to include the appropriate acknowledgements on reprinting and in the next update to the digital edition, as applicable.

Key: B = Below, C = Centre, T = Top, TL = Top Left, TR = Top right, BL = Below left, BR = Below right.

p. 10 (rubber): spaxiax/Shutterstock; p. 10 (pencil): duckycards/iStock/Getty Images; p. 10 (bag): Tpopova/iStockphoto/Getty Images; p. 10 (ruler): oku/Shutterstock; p. 10 (pencil): Mosutatsu/iStockphoto/Getty Images; p. 10: EuToch/iStockphoto/Getty Images; p. 26 (cat): photographer, loves art, lives in Kyoto/Moment/Getty Images; p. 26 (rat): Arathrael Photography/Moment/Getty Images; p. 27: Ulianna/iStock/Getty Images; p. 38: Tigatelu/iStock/Getty Images; p. 50 (TL): Steve Prezant/mage Source/Getty Images; p. 50 (TR): Compassionate Eye Foundation/DigitalVision/Getty Images; p. 53 (TR) © Cybernesco/iStockphoto; p. 53 (BL) © Riddy/iStockphoto; p. 53 (TC) © Alex White/Shutterstock; p. 53 (BC) © carlosalvarez/iStockphoto; p. 53 (TL) © tkemot/Shutterstock; p. 53 (BR) © Mike Flippo/Shutterstock; p. 56 (T): kenex/iStock/Getty Images; p. 56 (C): Ami-Rian/iStock/Getty Images; p. 56 (B): kenex/DigitalVision Vectors/Getty Images; p. 56 (dog): alexei_tm/iStock/Getty Images; p. 62 (castle): Mariusz Kluzniak/Moment Open/Getty Images; p. 62: Joff Lee/Photolibrary/Getty Images.

The following photographs on pages p.17, p.25, p.31, p.36, p.49 by were taken on commission by Stephen Bond for Cambridge University Press

The publishers are grateful to the following illustrators:

Clive Goodyer, Anna Hancock (Beehive), Marek Jagucki, Chris Lensch, Bernice Lum, Alan Rowe, David Semple